30-MINUTE
CHEMISTRY
PROJECTS

Anna Leigh

Lerner Publications ◆ Minneapolis

Official Licensed Product
Lerner Publications Company
A division of Lerner Publishing Group, Inc.
241 First Avenue North
Minneapolis, MN 55401 USA

For reading levels and more information, look up this title at www.lernerbooks.com.

Main body text set in Hoosker Don't.
Typeface provided by The Chank Company.

Library of Congress Cataloging-in-Publication Data

Names: Leigh, Anna, author.
Title: 30-minute chemistry projects / Anna Leigh.
Description: Minneapolis : Lerner Publications, [2019] | Series: 30-minute makers
   | Audience: Ages 7-11. | Audience: Grades 4 to 6. | Includes bibliographical
   references and index.
Identifiers: LCCN 2018016825 (print) | LCCN 2018026914 (ebook) | ISBN
   9781541542884 (eb pdf) |
   ISBN 9781541538931 (lb : alk. paper)
Subjects: LCSH: Chemistry—Experiments—Juvenile literature. | Science projects—
   Juvenile literature.
Classification: LCC QD43 (ebook) | LCC QD43 .L3545 2019 (print) | DDC 540.78—dc23

LC record available at https://lccn.loc.gov/2018016825

Manufactured in the United States of America
1-45076-35903-10/10/2018

CONTENTS

For even more chemistry projects, scan this QR code!

WHAT IS CHEMISTRY?

Chemistry is a kind of science that deals with the tiny particles that make up substances. Everything on Earth is made of molecules. How these molecules behave determines whether something is a solid, like an ice cube; a liquid, like water; or a gas, like steam.

When molecules change their behavior, substances can also change. For example, ice can melt to become liquid water. Molecules can react with one another to create new substances too, such as when you mix baking soda and vinegar and make lots and lots of foamy bubbles. There are many fun ways to explore chemistry. What will you discover?

BEFORE YOU GET STARTED

Ask an adult for permission before doing any projects. Some projects require knives, a stove, or substances such as bleach or borax and may require help from an adult. You can find most of these materials around your home or school. Other materials will be easy to find at a grocery store or pet store.

While doing these projects, make sure you have a workspace that can get wet or dirty, and always wear safety goggles when the instructions include them.

GLOW-IN-THE-DARK WATER

Have you ever seen water glow in the dark? Tonic water is a special kind of water that's a bit like soda. Shine a black light on it, and see what you see!

 **TIMEFRAME: 10 minutes**

MATERIALS

⇨ measuring cup

⇨ tonic water

⇨ clear, disposable plastic cup

⇨ ultraviolet black light

⇨ medicine dropper

⇨ bleach

⇨ spoon

SCIENCE TAKEAWAY

Tonic water contains a chemical called quinine that absorbs ultraviolet light and gives off blue light, so it appears to glow. Bleach breaks down the quinine molecules so they are no longer able to absorb ultraviolet light and give off blue light.

1. Pour 1 cup of tonic water into the plastic cup.

2. In a dark room, turn on the ultraviolet black light. Shine it on the cup. What do you see?

3. Use the medicine dropper to add 2 drops of bleach to the tonic water.

4. Stir the mixture, turn off the lights again, and shine the ultraviolet black light on the cup. Do you see a change in the tonic water?

5. If you do not see a change, try adding a few more drops of bleach. What happens?

LET'S MAKE OOBLECK!

What is **Oobleck?** It sounds kind of icky, and you definitely won't want to eat it. But you will want to play with this slippery, slimy stuff!

🕐 **TIMEFRAME: 20 to 30 minutes**

MATERIALS

⇨ measuring spoons

⇨ cornstarch

⇨ small bowl

⇨ mug

⇨ water

⇨ medicine dropper

⇨ fork

⇨ food coloring (optional)

SCIENCE TAKEAWAY

In solids, molecules are tightly packed together to hold a shape. In liquids, molecules can move over and around one another. Most liquids are runny and move out of the way when you press on them. Oobleck does not act like most liquids. It is a non-Newtonian liquid, which becomes solid when you press on it.

1 Add 1 tablespoon of cornstarch to the small bowl.

2 Fill the mug with water.

3 Use the medicine dropper to add 20 drops of water from the mug to the cornstarch. Stir the cornstarch and water with a fork to break up any clumps that have formed.

4 Repeat step 3 until you have added 100 drops. What does the mixture look like?

5 Add 10 more drops of water. Stir the mixture with a fork.

6 Repeat step 5 until the cornstarch mixture looks like a liquid. It will probably take about 150 to 170 drops of water. How would you describe the mixture now?

7 You have made Oobleck! Play with the Oobleck in the bowl. Squeeze it in your hand and scoop it with your fingers. If it feels chalky, add more water. If you want to color your Oobleck, add a few drops of food coloring.

MAKE YOUR OWN SLIME

Is Oobleck not quite slimy enough for you? Try out this recipe for another slippery substance!

⏱ **TIMEFRAME: 15 minutes**

MATERIALS

⇨ safety goggles

⇨ measuring cups

⇨ warm water

⇨ drinking glass

⇨ measuring spoons

⇨ borax powder

⇨ plastic spoon

⇨ marker

⇨ tape

⇨ white school glue

⇨ mixing bowl

⇨ food coloring (optional)

⇨ airtight container or plastic bag

SCIENCE TAKEAWAY

Slime, like Oobleck, is a non-Newtonian liquid. It doesn't act like typical solids or liquids. The long glue molecules and the borax link together to make larger polymers. These larger molecules do not slide past one another easily, making the slime feel more like a solid when you squeeze it.

1. Ask an adult to help you create a borax solution. Put on your safety goggles since borax can irritate the eyes. Add ½ cup of warm water to a drinking glass. Add ½ tablespoon of borax powder to the water. Stir the mixture until the solution looks clear. Use the marker and tape to label the glass "borax solution." Set the solution aside.

2. Pour ½ cup of glue and ¼ cup of warm water into a mixing bowl. To make colored slime, add a few drops of food coloring. Stir the mixture with the plastic spoon.

3. Add 5 tablespoons of the borax solution to your glue and water mixture and stir. Do you notice some of the mixture sticking to your spoon? Does it look like a solid or a liquid?

4. If your mixture is still watery, add ½ teaspoon of borax at a time until very little water is left.

5. Pick up the substance in your hands, and work it for about 1 minute. How does the slime feel? Does it seem like a liquid or a solid?

6. Try playing with your slime. Form it into a ball, pull on it, stretch it, and rip it. What happens? Does it feel as if you are playing with something solid or liquid?

7. To keep your slime soft, store it in an airtight container or plastic bag.

MAGIC DOUGH

The magic in this dough is actually just simple science! You'll never guess what happens when you mix oil and flour together.

TIMEFRAME: 15 minutes

MATERIALS

⇨ measuring cups

⇨ flour

⇨ mixing bowl

⇨ measuring spoons

⇨ cooking oil

⇨ small bowl

⇨ food coloring (optional)

⇨ fork

SCIENCE TAKEAWAY

Oil consists of long chains of molecules. When oil coats the flour, the polymers grab on to one another and make the flour stick together so you can mold the magic dough into shapes.

1. Measure 1 cup of flour into the mixing bowl.

2. Pour 2 tablespoons of oil into a separate small bowl. To make colored magic dough, mix in a few drops of food coloring.

3. Slowly add 1 tablespoon of the oil to the bowl of flour. Use a fork to mix the oil into the flour until the oil is no longer visible and there are no big clumps of flour.

4. Add another tablespoon of oil to the flour. Mix the oil and flour with a fork.

5. Use your fingers to mix and squeeze the flour with the oil. What does it feel like? How is it different from the flour you started with? What happens when you squeeze the flour in your fist?

6. If the flour does not hold its shape when you squeeze it, add ½ tablespoon of oil. The dough should feel dry to the touch and hold its shape when squeezed.

TURN MILK INTO PLASTIC

Can you believe that you can make plastic out of regular milk?
Seems impossible, doesn't it? Try it out for yourself!

🕐 **TIMEFRAME: 30 minutes**

MATERIALS

⇨ measuring cups

⇨ milk

⇨ saucepan

⇨ stove

⇨ measuring spoons

⇨ white vinegar

⇨ mug

⇨ spoon

⇨ paper towels

SCIENCE TAKEAWAY

Vinegar is an acid. When you add it to milk, the casein molecules in milk
unfold into polymers, creating curds. When you clump the curds together,
you can mold them into shapes.

1. With an adult's help, heat 1 cup of milk in a pan on the stove until the milk is steaming.

2. Add 4 teaspoons of vinegar to a mug. Then add the hot milk. You should see the milk form white clumps, or curds. Stir the mixture with a spoon.

3. Stack four layers of paper towels on a hard surface.

4. When the milk and vinegar mixture has cooled, pour it through a strainer to catch the curds. Place the curds on top of the paper towels.

5. Fold the edges of the paper towels over the curds, and press down to soak up extra liquid from the curds.

6. Combine all the curds together into a ball. This is your plastic.

7. Try molding the plastic into a shape. Then leave your creation to dry for 48 hours. Once it is dry, the plastic will be hard.

FOAMY SNOW

Make your own snow. Then watch what happens when you pour vinegar all over it!

🕐 **TIMEFRAME: 30 minutes**

MATERIALS

⇨ measuring cups

⇨ baking soda

⇨ 2 large plastic containers

⇨ measuring spoons

⇨ water

⇨ dishwashing soap

⇨ vinegar

SCIENCE TAKEAWAY

When baking soda and vinegar combine, a chemical reaction produces bubbles of carbon dioxide gas. Soap gets between the molecules of the liquid to trap the air bubbles and create foam.

1. Add 1 cup of baking soda to each plastic container.

2. Add 3 tablespoons of water to one of the containers. Mix the water and baking soda into a dough. The dough should feel soft and not too sticky or crumbly. Add a little more water or baking soda until the dough reaches the right texture.

3. Add 1 teaspoon of dishwashing soap to the second container of baking soda. Then add 3 tablespoons of water. Mix the ingredients together into a dough.

4. Keep both doughs in their separate containers. Play with both. How do the doughs feel similar or different?

5. Make a creation such as a snowperson or other creature out of both doughs.

6. Pour ½ cup of vinegar over your first dough creation. What happens? What do you see and hear?

7. Repeat step 6 with the second dough creation.

8. Pour ½ cup of water over what is left of the first creation. What happens?

9. Repeat step 8 with the second creation.

HOMEMADE LAVA LAMP

Lava lamps are filled with liquid and wax that forms fascinating floating bubbles. Find out how to make your own colorful floating bubbles with this project!

🕐 **TIMEFRAME: 10 to 20 minutes**

MATERIALS

⇨ water

⇨ food coloring

⇨ 2 identical tall jars

⇨ vegetable oil

⇨ large bowl

⇨ refrigerator

⇨ knife

⇨ cutting board

⇨ antacid tablet

⇨ timer or stopwatch

⇨ ruler

SCIENCE TAKEAWAY

The ingredients in antacids combine with water to produce carbon dioxide gas. Oil does not react with the antacid in this way. When the tablet hits the water at the bottom of the jar, bubbles form. Gas is lighter than liquid, so the colored bubbles rise up through the oil.

1. Add 1 to 2 inches (2.5 to 5 cm) of water and 5 drops of food coloring to each jar.

2. Fill each jar at least three-quarters full of vegetable oil. Put the caps on tightly.

3. Place one of the jars in a large bowl of hot water to warm it. Place the other jar in the refrigerator to make it cold.

4. While the jars are heating and cooling, cut an antacid tablet into quarters.

5. Drop a piece of the antacid tablet into the warm jar. Wait for the tablet to fall through the oil.

6. Start the timer as soon as the tablet reaches the water and begins reacting. How long does it take the tablet to disappear? How does the lava lamp look?

7. Repeat step 4 with the cold jar. How were the two reactions similar or different?

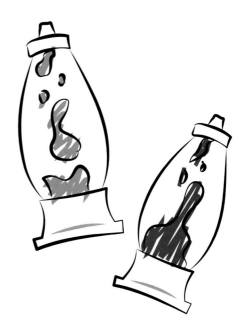

CANDY RAINBOW

Make colorful designs out of sugar and water!

🕐 **TIMEFRAME: 20 minutes**

MATERIALS

⇨ hard-shelled colored candies

⇨ small plate

⇨ drinking glass

⇨ warm water

⇨ paper towels

⇨ measuring spoons

⇨ sugar

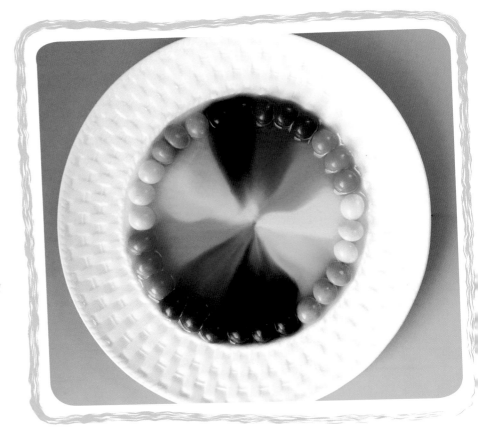

SCIENCE TAKEAWAY

Molecules move from areas of high concentration to areas of low concentration. When water touches the candy, the sugar coating dissolves and the sugar molecules move toward the center. The dye spread more slowly the second time because the concentration of sugar was more even on the plate.

1. Arrange the pieces of candy in a circle around the inner rim of the plate. Use at least 2 different colors, alternating them in groups of 2 or 3.

2. Fill the glass with warm water. Slowly pour the water into the middle of the plate until it partially covers the candy.

3. Watch the plate closely for a few minutes. What happens?

4. Empty and dry off the plate.

5. Repeat step 1. Then place ¼ teaspoon of sugar in the middle of the plate.

6. Slowly pour water near the center of the plate (but not directly onto the sugar).

7. Watch the plate closely for a few minutes. What happens this time?

23

TIE-DYE T-SHIRTS

Tie-dye is a fun way to make colorful patterns and designs on your clothes. Try this method, which uses permanent markers and a special liquid.

🕐 **TIMEFRAME: 30 minutes**

MATERIALS

⇨ newspapers

⇨ white T-shirt

⇨ 2 or more plastic cups

⇨ 2 or more rubber bands

⇨ colorful assortment of permanent markers

⇨ medicine dropper

⇨ water

⇨ rubbing alcohol

SCIENCE TAKEAWAY

The ink used in permanent markers does not dissolve in water. The ink does dissolve in rubbing alcohol. This is why the ink stays in place when you drop water on it but runs when you use the rubbing alcohol.

1 Cover your work surface with a few layers of newspaper. Lay your T-shirt over the newspapers.

2 Wherever you want to make a design on the T-shirt (in at least two different places), place a plastic cup under the shirt, and loop a rubber band around the edge of the cup. You should have a flat, tight circle of the fabric stretched over the cup opening.

3 Using the permanent markers, draw some colorful designs in each circle you made with the cups.

4 Use the medicine dropper to drop a few drops of water onto the center of one of the circles. What happens when the water touches the ink?

5 Drop several more drops of water onto the circle until it is thoroughly damp.

6 Use the medicine dropper to drop a few drops of rubbing alcohol onto the center of one of the other flat circles. What happens to the ink when the alcohol touches it?

7 Drop several more drops of alcohol onto the same circle until it is thoroughly damp.

8 Compare the two circles. Which looks better?

9 Let the circles dry, and decorate the whole shirt with whichever liquid gave you the best results.

CLEAN WATER

Have you ever poured tap water through a water filter before drinking it? Do you know what these filters do? Find out with this fun project that filters a colored drink.

🕐 **TIMEFRAME: 30 minutes**

MATERIALS

⇨ permanent marker

⇨ 5 disposable plastic cups

⇨ 4 coffee filters

⇨ measuring spoons

⇨ granular activated carbon, rinsed

⇨ colored sports drink or soda

⇨ timer

1. Use the permanent marker to label the plastic cups 0, 1a, 1b, 2a, and 2b.

2. Prepare 2 double-layered coffee filters by inserting a filter into another to form 2 layers.

3. Add 1½ tablespoons of activated carbon to cups 1a and 2a.

4. Add 3 tablespoons of the sports drink or soda to cup 0. What does the drink look like? How does it smell?

5 Add 3 tablespoons of the sports drink to cups 1a and 2a. Swirl each cup to make sure the solution mixes well.

6 Start the timer for 5 minutes.

7 Hold one double-layered coffee filter over cup 1b. When the timer goes off after 5 minutes, pour the contents of cup 1a into the filter. Collect the liquid in cup 1b.

8 Start the timer for 20 minutes. While waiting, swirl cup 2a occasionally.

9 After 20 minutes, hold the second double-layered coffee filter over cup 2b. Pour the liquid from cup 2a into the filter and collect the liquid in cup 2b.

10 Compare the contents of cup 0, 1b, and 2b. How did the sports drink change over time? How does the liquid in each cup look and smell?

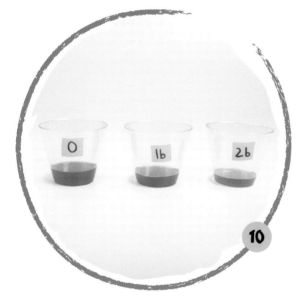

SCIENCE TAKEAWAY

Activated carbon has many tiny pores that soak up liquids. When you add activated carbon to a sports drink, an interaction happens that traps the flavor and color molecules in the drink to the surface of the pores. This is called adsorption.

CREATIVE CHEMISTRY

Make sure to clean up your workspace after every project. Throw away any creations you don't want to keep—but don't pour them down the drain! Oil and Oobleck can clog your pipes!

If you want to learn more about these projects, do them again with a few changes. What happens if you add soap to your slime? What if you pour soda over your foamy snow creation instead of vinegar? Try filtering a different kind of drink. Does one drink work better? There's lots to find out about chemistry!

For even more chemistry projects, scan this QR code!

GLOSSARY

absorb: to take in

acid: a chemical that has a sour taste

adsorption: when a thin layer of molecules sticks to the solid or liquid it is touching

casein: a protein in milk used for making paint and plastic

chemical reaction: a process in which one or more substances are changed into one or more different substances

concentration: the amount of something in one place

curd: a thick substance that forms in sour milk and that makes cheese

dissolve: to become part of a liquid

molecule: the smallest piece a material can be divided into without changing how it behaves

non-Newtonian liquid: a liquid that temporarily acts like a solid when you put it under pressure, such as by squeezing it

polymer: a long chain-like molecule made up of a repeated pattern of smaller molecules

ultraviolet light: rays of light that cannot be seen

FURTHER INFORMATION

For more information and projects, visit **Science Buddies** at **https://www.sciencebuddies.org/.**

Ives, Rob. *Fun Experiments with Matter: Invisible Ink, Giant Bubbles, and More.* Minneapolis: Hungry Tomato, 2018.

Leigh, Anna. *30-Minute Edible Science Projects.* Minneapolis: Lerner Publications, 2019.

Slingerland, Janet. *Explore Atoms and Molecules! With 25 Great Projects.* White River Junction, VT: Nomad, 2017.

INDEX

PHOTO ACKNOWLEDGMENTS

The images in this book are used with the permission of: Design element (pencil) © primiaou/Shutterstock Images, pp. 8, 10, 12, 14, 16, 18, 20, 22, 24, 29; © Visual Generation/Shutterstock Images, pp. 1 (clock), 30 (clock); © Minur/Shutterstock Images, pp. 1 (pitcher, beaker), 10 (bowl), 11 (corn starch, water beaker), 14 (bowl), 15 (oil, flour), 26 (pitcher, cup); © Squirrell/Shutterstock Images, pp. 1 (saucepan), 17 (pan, colander); © Artur Balytskyi/Shutterstock Images, pp. 1 (stopwatch), 28 (stopwatch); © Sashatigar/Shutterstock Images, pp. 1 (children with goggles), 12 (girl with goggles), 13 (boy with goggles); © BlueHorse_pl/Shutterstock Images, p. 4 (hand with ice); © jarabee123/Shutterstock Images, p. 5 (girl with pink slime); © andras_csontos/Shutterstock Images, p. 6 (girl with green slime); © wavebreakmedia/Shutterstock Images, p. 7 (boy cooking); © Mighty Media, Inc., pp. 7 (measuring cups, spoons, food coloring, eyedropper, safety goggles, saucepan, red bowl, dinner knife), 8–29 (project photos), 20 (lava lamp), 21 (lava lamps), 22 (rainbow, candies) 23 (candies), 24 (T-shirt), 27 (cups), 29 (cups); © VectorShow/Shutterstock Images, p. 9 (bottles, cups); © Nina Puankova/Shutterstock Images, p. 18 (snowflakes); © Tiwat K/Shutterstock Images, p. 31 (computer)

Front cover: © Artur Balytskyi/Shutterstock Images (brain); © primiaou/Shutterstock Images (light bulb); © STILLFX/Shutterstock Images (background); © Tom and Kwikki/Shutterstock Images (chemistry set, molecules); © Visual Generation/Shutterstock Images (clock)

Back cover: © DariaRoozen/Shutterstock Images (question mark); © primiaou/Shutterstock Images (molecules, pencil); © STILLFX/Shutterstock Images (background); © Tiwat K/Shutterstock Images (H2O); © Tom and Kwikki/Shutterstock Images (beaker)